Penguins:

100+ Amazing & Interesting Facts that Everyone Should Know

By Bandana Ojha

All rights reserved. This book or any portion thereof may not be reproduced or used in any manner without the express written permission of the author.

Copyright © 2020 By the author.

Introduction

"Penguins: 100+ Amazing & Interesting Facts that Everyone Should Know is a book for all kids. The young readers will get a fun and fascinating way to find out more about some of the world's cutest animals. This informative book will help children to learn more about Penguins. and to know what makes penguins unique members of the animal kingdom. With amazing images this Penguins book will cover some interesting insights about Penguins, where penguins live, the true reason they have that tuxedo look, how they survive such extreme weather conditions, the many different species of penguins such as Emperor penguin, Blue penguin Adelie penguin, Macaroni penguin, Rockhopper penguin, African penguin, yellow eyed penguin, Chinstrap penguin and much more. All about the smallest, fastest, tallest, how they communicate, when they discovered- bits of information which can touch the kid's inquisitive mind.

1. Penguins are birds with black and white feathers and a funny waddle. But unlike most birds, penguins are not able to fly in the air and mostly live in the Southern Hemisphere.

2. 17 species of Penguins are there. Out of the 17 species, 13 are either threatened or endangered, with some on the brink of extinction.

3. Most penguins are found in South Africa, New Zealand, Chili, Antarctica, Argentina, and Australia.

4. Penguins live up to 80 percent of their lives in the ocean.

5. Penguins lost their ability to fly millions of year ago. However, they are the fastest-swimming and deepest-diving species of any bird.

6. Penguins do not live in the best habitats for finding nesting material, so they make their nest with what they can find.

7. Penguin nesting areas are called "rookeries" and may contain thousands of pairs of birds. Each penguin has a distinct call, which allows individual penguins to find their mates and chicks even in the largest groups.

8. A baby Penguin is called a Chick.

9. Baby penguins assemble group is called a Crèches.

10. Rockhopper penguins build their nests on steep rocky areas.

11. Adelies and Chinstrap penguins use rocks to build their nests. The perfect rock is a rare commodity for these birds. They will often fight over or steal each other's stones.

12. Among all species the largest penguins are the Emperor Penguins. They can be 3ft 7 inches tall and weigh

75 pounds. Emperor Penguins live in Antarctica.

13. Magellanic penguins dig burrows under the ground to form huge cities.

14. Emperor penguins are easily identifiable by their size and the orange "glow" on their cheeks.

15. Most penguin species lay two eggs at a time, but due to the difficulty of raising chicks in such a harsh climate, the Emperor penguin only lays one egg.

16. Most penguin species take turns warming the egg, but it is up to the male Emperor penguin to do all the work once the egg is laid.

17. The male stands with the egg on his feet and does this for up to 9 weeks, without food, waiting for the chick to hatch.

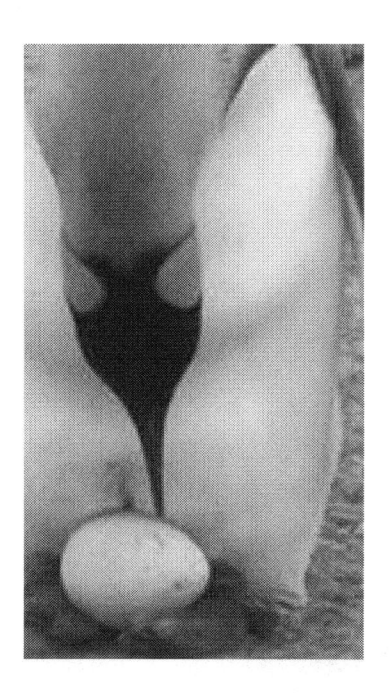

18. During this time, the male may lose up to half its body weight.

19. Adelie penguins were named after the wife of a French explorer in the 1830s. They are about 2 feet tall and weigh 8 or 9 pounds. One way to distinguish them from the other penguins is by their all black head and the white ring around their eye.

20. Adelie Penguins build their nests of stones on the rocky beaches of Antarctica, jealously guarding and often fighting over the best rocks.

21. Researcher believe that male adelie penguins give their females rocks as gifts.

22. They raise their beaks and spread their wings to communicate with each other.

23. Penguins do not live in the wild in any location in the Northern Hemisphere.

24. Gentoo penguins are the fastest penguins of all species.

25. Gentoo penguins are easily identifiable by the wide white stripe over the top of their head.

26. They live on many of the islands of the Antarctic region, but the main colony is on the Falklands.

27. They are about 3 feet tall and weigh about 13 pounds. Their diet consists of krill and some small fish.

28. Gentoo penguins make nests on the inland grasslands. They pile stones, grass and sticks to create a circular nest. Gentoo penguins also fight over stones for nesting.

29. The King penguin is the second largest penguin and looks somewhat like the Emperor penguin. They are

about 3 feet tall and weigh up to 35 pounds.

30. King penguins mainly eat fish and some squid and crustaceans.

31. Like the Emperor penguin, the King penguin hatches only one chick at a time.

32. King penguins have orange spots near their ears and on the neck.

33. They are found on many sub-Antarctic islands including Crozet, Prince Edward, Kerguelen, South Georgia and Macquarie island.

34. The Macaroni penguins were so named because the yellow and black feathers sticking out of the side of their heads.

35. Magellanic penguins were named after the explorer Ferdinand Magellan who first saw them in 1519 on his first voyage around the tip of South America.

36. Magellanic penguins are about 2 feet, 3 inches tall and weigh 9 pounds. They are the largest of the warm weather penguins.

37. They live on the coast of the Argentina, Chile and the Falkland Islands.

38. Like the Macaroni penguins, the Rockhopper penguins have decorative

feather tufts on their heads -- theirs are yellow in color.

39. The Specialty about the rockhopper penguin is that they keep both feet together when hopping. Using this method, they can hop up to four or five feet and they hop up steep, rocky slopes to their nests above sea level.

40. The rarest penguin in the world is the Yellow-eyed Penguin, with only around 5,000 living in the wild.

41. They live along the southeastern coast of New Zealand and nearby islands.

42. The yellow-eyed penguins have a band of yellow feathers going from the bill, circling the eyes and up around the head.

43. African penguins have a black upside-down U-shape on their neck with black speckles on their chest. They are about 2 feet tall and weigh between 7 and 11 pounds.

44. African penguins are also known as the Blackfoot penguin.

45. African penguins live and breed on the coast of South Africa. People have hunted these penguins so much that their numbers declined from at least one million to about 150,000.

46. They are now a protected species but are still caused trouble by oil spills off the coast of Africa.

47. Chinstrap penguins get their name from the small black band that runs under their chin. They are about 2 feet tall and weigh about 10 pounds. They feed on krill and fish.

48. Chinstrap penguins are the most common penguins with a population of about 13 million.

49. They often live on large icebergs on the open ocean in the Antarctic region.

50. A Chinstrap Penguins is called "Stone Cracker" penguin.

51. Size and the markings on heads and necks. make them different from various species of Penguin.

52. As soon as the egg is laid (penguins lay one or two eggs at a time), the female dashes out for dinner, leaving the male to watch the nest.

53. When the female returns (it can take up to two weeks for her to come back) it's the male's turn to head out for food, leaving the female with the egg.

54. When the chick hatches, it immediately starts calling so that its parents will learn to recognize its voice.

55. Once the chick is strong enough, both parents head for the ocean at the

same time. The chicks are left in a group together (sort of like a daycare).

56. When the penguin parents return with dinner, they recognize their chick by its voice.

57. Little Blue Penguins live in Southern Australia and New Zealand. Another name of Little blue penguin is the fairy penguin.

58. They sing and use body movement to communicate with each other.

59. Blue Penguin is the smallest Penguin among all species. It stands

about 35 cm tall and weighs about 1.2 kg.

60. Penguins do not have teeth. Instead they use their beak to grab and hold wiggling prey. They have spines on the roof of their beak to help them get a good grip.

61. Little Penguins consume about their body weight every day. Major food

items are small schooling fish (76%), squid (24%) and occasional krill (<1%).

62. The yellow-eyed penguin is very tenacious when foraging for food. It will dive as deep as 120 meters (393.70 feet) up to 200 times a day looking for fish.

63. Penguins swallow pebbles and stones as well as their food. Scientists

believe that the stones may help grind up and digest their food. The stones may also add enough extra weight to help penguins dive deeper.

64. Penguins undergo a process called catastrophic molting, when they replace all their feathers in the space of a few weeks. During this time, they cannot enter the water, so they need to have accumulated enough fat to fast through this period.

65. Penguins can stay underwater for 10-15 minutes before coming to the surface to breathe. Penguins cannot breathe underwater.

66. Penguins swim so fast that they can propel themselves over 7 feet (2

meters) above water. They used to cut through waves like dolphins or porpoises.

67. Most birds replace their feathers gradually over the course of the year, while penguins must go through this process all at once.

68. Generally, penguins are not sexually dimorphic, meaning male and female penguins look alike.

69. Penguins ingest a lot of seawater while hunting for fish, but a special gland behind their eyes—the supraorbital gland—filters out the saltwater from their blood stream. Penguins excrete it through their beaks, or by sneezing.

70. Penguin parents—both male and female—care for their young for several months until the chicks are strong enough to hunt for food on their own.

71. Many bird species are adapted to flying by having hollow bones, whereas

penguins have dense bones, which makes diving easier.

72. Chinstrap Penguins is the boldest and most aggressive of all penguins.

73. Scientists discovered that a primary reason penguin can swim so fast is that they have a special "bubble boost." When penguins fluff their feathers, they

release bubbles that reduce the density of the water around them. The bubbles act as lubrication that decreases water viscosity and easier for Penguins to swim fast.

74. Penguins often move across ice by gliding across the ice on their stomachs.

75. All penguins live in the Southern Hemisphere, from Antarctica to the warmer waters of the Galapagos Islands near the equator. They can be found on every continent in the Southern Hemisphere. No penguins live at the North Pole.

76. When a mother emperor penguin loses her chick, she tries to steal another chick.

77. The average life expectancy of penguins is probably 15 to 20 years. Some species live considerably longer and some live shorter. Emperor penguin lives up to 20 yrs. and little blue penguin lives up to 6 yrs.

78. An Emperor penguin can hold its breath for 20 mins.

79. Penguins have more feathers than most other birds, averaging approximately 70 feathers per square inch. The Emperor Penguin has the most of any bird, at around 100 feathers per one square inch.

80. Small Penguins typically dive up to 1-3 mins.

81. Large Penguins typically dive up to 20-30 mins.

82. Dense outer feathers keeps penguin's outer skin dry.

83. The only time penguins are airborne is when they leap out of the water. Penguins will often do this to get a gulp of air before diving back down for fish.

84. Just one species of penguin naturally appears above the equator that is the Galapagos penguin.

85. The name penguin was originally given to an unrelated bird species – the now-extinct great auk, which was a large, flightless, black, and white bird.

86. The fastest underwater swimming bird is the Gentoo Penguin, able to swim up to 22 mph (36 km/h).

87. Penguins all hunt for food in the same way. They can either catch it out of the water, or scrape the smaller food, like krill, off the underside of the ice.

88. When penguin chicks hatch, they are not waterproof, so they must stay out of the ocean. They depend on their parents to bring them food and to keep them warm until waterproof feathers replace their fluffy down coats

89. The adult penguin swallows the food and saves it for later changing it into a form that the chicks can eat.

90. The parent catches the fish, krill or squid, digests it or holds it in for a while, then when it is ready, it regurgitates the food into its beak, and then uses its beak as a kind of spoon to place the food into the baby penguin's mouth.

91. Some breeds of penguins can completely digest their fish and krill before they feed it to their chicks.

When this happens, a form of oil is made from all the nutrients from the food. This process takes several days to occur. The penguin then gives that fish "milk" to its young.

92. A group of Penguin in land is called a Waddle.

93. Penguins cannot breathe underwater, though they are able to hold their breath for a long time.

94. A group of Penguin in water is called a Raft.

95. Penguins usually enter and leave the sea in large groups. Scientists believe this is for "safety in numbers." By blending into a crowd, an individual penguin may avoid catching the attention of a predator.

96. Penguins huddle together with their friends to keep warm. Emperor penguins have developed a social behavior that when they get cold, they huddle together in groups that may comprise several thousand penguins.

97. Penguins can control the blood flow to their extremities to reduce the amount of blood that gets cold, but not enough so that their extremities freeze.

98. Penguins tightly packed feathers overlap to provide waterproofing and warmth. They coat their feathers with oil from a gland near the tail to increase impermeability.

99. Penguins' eyes work better under water than they do in air. Many scientists believe penguins are extremely short-sighted on land.

100. A penguin's normal body temperature is approximately 100-degree Fahrenheit.

101. Larger penguins usually live in cooler regions. Smaller penguins are typically found in more temperate and tropical climates

102. The penguins are not without protection though. Their white bellies blend with the snow and sunlight making it difficult for an underwater predator to see them.

103. Penguins are a food source for several marine mammals, especially leopard seals. These seals hide under ice flows and wait for their prey.

104. Other marine mammal predators are sea lions and orcas.

105. Penguins also have several on-land predators like ferrets, cats, snakes, lizards, foxes, and rats.

106. Penguins are also eaten by several birds like the Australian sea eagle and the Skua. The penguin's black backs blend against the dark ocean water,

making it more difficult to spot them from above.

Please check this out:

Our other best-selling books for kids are-

Know about Sharks: 100+ Amazing Facts That Everyone Should Know

Know About Whales: 100+ Amazing Facts That Everyone Should Know

Know About Dinosaurs: 100+ Amazing Facts That Everyone Should Know

Know About Kangaroos: 100+ Amazing Facts That Everyone Should Know

Know About Penguins: 100+ Amazing Facts That Everyone Should Know

Know About Dolphins: 100+ Amazing Facts That Everyone Should Know

All About Elephant: 100+ Amazing Facts That Everyone Should Know

All About New York: 100+ Amazing Facts That Everyone Should Know

All About New Jersey: 100+ Amazing Facts That Everyone Should Know

All About Massachusetts: 100+ Amazing Facts That Everyone Should Know

All About Florida: 100+ Amazing Facts That Everyone Should Know

All About California: 100+ Amazing Facts That Everyone Should Know

All About Arizona: 100+ Amazing Facts with Pictures

All About Texas: 100+ Amazing Facts That Everyone Should Know

All About Minnesota: 100+ Amazing Facts That Everyone Should Know

All About Italy: 100+ Amazing Facts That Everyone Should Know

All About France: 100+ Amazing Facts That Everyone Should Know

All About Japan: 100+ Amazing Facts That Everyone Should Know

100 Amazing Quiz Q & A About Penguin: Never Known Before Penguin Facts

Most Popular Animal Quiz book for Kids: 100 amazing animal facts

Quiz Book for Kids: Science, History, Geography, Biology, Computer & Information Technology

English Grammar for Kids: Most Easy Way to learn English Grammar

Solar System & Space Science- Quiz for Kids: What You Know About Solar System

English Grammar Practice Book for elementary kids: 1000+ Practice Questions with Answers

A to Z of English Tense

My First Fruits

Printed in Great Britain
by Amazon